BIA DA AIKILI:

DA EKININEI BU AWARIMO HAI A~ ANXIHI BU'WAYA KEI TEKETA KEI DA ANXIHI BU.

PARA MI HIJO:

ESPERO QUE LLEGUES A AMARTE TANTO COMO YO TE AMO.

FOR MY SON:

I HOPE YOU GROW UP TO LOVE YOURSELF AS MUCH AS I LOVE YOU.

DA TRAHA YATAYA.

SOY VALIENTE.

I AM BRAVE.

A

DA TRAHA OKOLO'AKI.

SOY DOTADO.

I AM GIFTED.

DA AHUIKI XAAPAI'NO!

¡MI VOZ IMPORTA!

MY VOICE MATTERS!

OMA TOMAKU AHUBO,
DA TRAHA KATIKUWA'LO.

CON CADA RESPIRA,
SOY MÁS FUERTE.

WITH EVERY BREATH,
I AM STRONGER.

DA TALATA'U LE ALU KA YARUBE
DA ANUDAHA A~ KOROKOA.

MI ALEGRÍA ESTÁ EN LA FORMA
EN QUE ELIJO PENSAR.

MY JOY IS IN THE WAY
I CHOOSE TO THINK.

DA MUKA KONA AITA'NI DA TRAHA AWUNIKIRA'KI.

CAMINARÉ SABIENDO QUE ESTOY PROTEGIDO.

I WILL WALK KNOWING I'M PROTECTED.

DA TRAHA ABAN OMA AKUAIBAWA KENA AKUAIBAWA LE ABAN OMA DAKA.

SOY UNO CON LA NATURALEZA Y LA NATURALEZA ES UNA CONMIGO.

I AM ONE WITH NATURE AND NATURE IS ONE WITH ME.

DA TRAHA KOHUYA.
YO SOY SUFICIENTE.
I AM ENOUGH.
A

DA HIDUADA
ALU DA'WAYA.

YO CREO EN MI MISMO.
I BELIEVE IN MYSELF.

DA IYARA AINAKA HAMABURUKU
DA SURU DA KOROKO A~.

PUEDO LOGRAR CUALQUIER COSA
QUE ME PROPONGA.

I CAN ACHIEVE ANYTHING I SET
MY MIND TO.

DA UBARADAN LE IBEKEBA TAN KI'TUKU AINAKA'ISA'GEI'NO.

MI FUTURO ESTÁ LLENO DE INFINITAS POSIBILIDADES.

MY FUTURE IS FULL OF ENDLESS POSSIBILITIES.

DA HEBEYO'NO DO TOKABU
INURAWA'NI HAI ALUWABU TAN DAKA.

MIS ANCESTROS SIEMPRE ESTÁN
SURGIENDO DENTRO DE MI.

MY ANCESTORS ARE FOREVER RISING
UP INSIDE OF ME.

ABOUT HIWATAHIA

Hiwatahia Hekexi Taino Arawak is a modern Tainan language reconstructed by merging recorded and continuing Taino words with words from the closest Tamaipurean Arawak languages such as Lokono, Wayu, Paraujano, Baniwa, Tariana, Wapishana and Garifuna. These languages have the closest cognates to Taino dialects. The language was founded by Kasike Jorge Baracutay Estevez and modified with the assistance of Tukada'lo Jessie Hurani Marrero. Together with Higuayagua language teams, the language has taken a life of its own.

Our goal is to create an autonomous speech for our people. Naturally we sought advice from some of the top Arawak linguists such as Alexandra Aikhenvald, Konrad Rybka, and others. In addition, we collobrated with Native Arawak Speakers. The effort actually began some 35 years ago, when Estevez began "collecting" Taino words from across the Caribbean. However with the help of our Languages teams and watchful eye of Jessie Hurani, in four years we were able to publish the work and begin teaching classes to our people. This is how Hiwatahia was born.

This work is not the revival of Ancient Taino languages. It is the beginning of a new language for the descendants of the Taino peoples. The approach is realistic and honest about its dimensions and limitations. This language is a beginning, and as our people continue to use it, it will continue to grow.

HIGUAYAGUA LANGUAGE TEAM

Founder of Hiwatahia
Kacike Jorge Baracutay Estevez

Director of Language
Jessie Hurani Marrero

Language Technologies Director
Alexander Adams

Language Teachers
Kalichi Lamar, Ra Ruiz Leon, Yal Quinones, Nelson Zayas

DEFINITIONS & PRONUNCIATIONS

A~ *conj.(Ah)* - To
Aban *(Ah-bahn)* - One
Ahubo *n.(Ah-hoo-boh)* - Breath
Ahuiki *n./v.(Ah-hoo-ee-kee)* - Voice
Ainaka *v.(Ah-ee-nah-kah)* - Achieve
Ainaka'isa'gei'no *n.(Ah-een-ah-kah-ee-sah-geh-ee-noh)* - Possibilities
Aita'ni *adj./v.(Ah-ee-tah-nee)* - Knowing
Akuaibawa *n.(Ah-koo-ah-ee-bah-wah)* - Nature
Alu *prep.(Ah-loo)* - In
Aluwabu *adj./n./prep.(Ah-loo-way-boo)* - Inside
Anudaha *v.(Ah-noo-dah-hah)* - Choose
Awunikira'ki *adj./v.(Ah-woo-nee-kee-rah-kee)* - Protected
Da *pron.(Dah)* - I, Me, Mine
Daka *pron.(Dah-kah)* - I, Me, Mine
Da'waya *pron.(Dah-wah-yah)* - Myself
Do *v.(Doh)* - Are
Hai *adj.adv./prep.(Hah-ee)* - Up
Hamaburuku *pron.(Hah-mah-boo-roo-koo)* - Anything
Hebeyo'no *n.(Heh-bey-yoh-noh)* - Ancestors
Hiudada *v.(Hee-doo-ah-dah)* - Believe
Ibekaba *adj.(Ee-beh-key-bah)* - Full
Inuaraw'ni *adj./v.(Ee-noo-rah-way-nee)* - Rising
Iyara *v.(Ee-yah-rah)* - Can (ability)
Ka *art.(Kah)* - The
Katikuwa'lo *adj.(Kah-tee-koo-wah-loh)* - Stronger
Kena *conj.(Keh-nah)* - And
Ki'tuku *n./v.(Kee-too-koo)* - Endless
Kohuya *adj./adv.(Koh-hoo-yah)* - Enough
Kona *v.(Koh-nah)* - Walk
Koroko *n./v.(Koh-roh-koh)* - Mind
Korokoa *v.(Koh-roh-koh-ah)* - Think
Le *v.(Leh)* - Is
Muka *v.(Moo-kah)* - Will
Okolo'aki *adj./v.(Oh-koh-loh-ah-kee)* - Gifted
Oma *prep.(Oh-mah)* - With
Suru *n./v. (Soo-roo)* - Set
Talata'u *n.(Tah-lah-tah-oo)* - Joy
Tan *prep.(Tahn)* - Of
Tokabu *adv.(Toh-kah-boo)* - Always
Tomaku *adj.(Toh-mah-koo)* - Every
Traha *v.(Trah-hah)* - Am
Ubaradan *n.(Oo-bah-rah-dahn)* - Future
Xaapai'no *v.(Shah-ah-pah-ee-noh)* - Matters
Yarube *n.(Yah-roo-beh)* - Way (manner)
Yataya *adj.(Yah-tah-yah)* - Brave

Made in the USA
Columbia, SC
24 October 2024